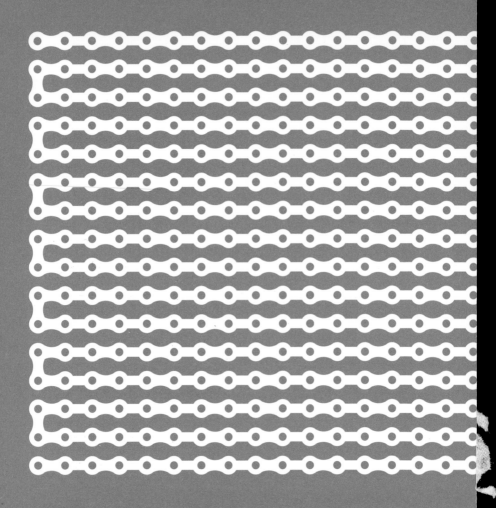

CYCLING

LET'S GET QUIZZICAL

GWION PRYDDERCH

SUMMERSDALE PUBLISHERS LTD

46 WEST STREET

CHICHESTER

WEST SUSSEX

PO19 1RP

UK

WWW.SUMMERSDALE.COM

PRINTED AND BOUND IN CHINA

ISBN: 978-1-84953-611-0

SUBSTANTIAL DISCOUNTS ON BULK QUANTITIES OF SUMMERSDALE BOOKS ARE AVAILABLE TO CORPORATIONS, PROFESSIONAL ASSOCIATIONS AND OTHER ORGANISATIONS. FOR DETAILS CONTACT NICKY DOUGLAS BY TELEPHONE: +44 (0) 1243 756902, FAX: +44 (0) 1243 786300 OR EMAIL: NICKY@SUMMERSDALE.COM

THIS PAIR ONLY APPEARS ONCE ON THE OPPOSITE PAGE

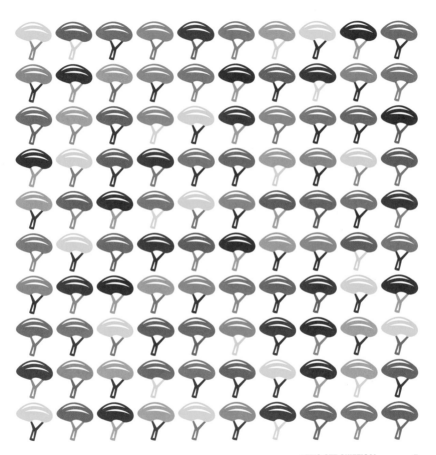

WHAT PERCENTAGE OF DUTCH PEOPLE OVER THE AGE OF 15 OWN A BIKE?

A) 56.2

B) 70

C) 87.5

BICYCLE PARTS

SADDLE
HANDLEBARS
FORK
HUB
CHAINRING
TYRE
WHEEL
BRAKE
GEAR
PEDAL
SPOKE

H	W	E	U	T	O	E	P	A	S
J	A	H	G	L	L	F	G	H	D
K	O	N	E	D	I	E	N	U	P
N	P	E	D	A	L	K	I	B	M
Y	H	A	E	L	B	A	R	V	C
W	S	R	D	S	E	R	N	G	A
F	Y	P	L	M	E	B	I	E	R
T	D	A	O	O	I	U	A	A	G
S	F	O	R	K	N	O	H	R	H
B	M	A	I	O	E	P	C	R	S

IN 1954, CROWDS SPAT AT ITALIAN CYCLIST FAUSTO COPPI DURING THE GIRO D'ITALIA BECAUSE:

A) HE REFUSED TO SHAKE THE POPE'S HAND BEFORE THE START OF THE RACE

B) HIS EXTRAMARITAL AFFAIR HAD BECOME PUBLIC

C) HIS BICYCLE WAS DECORATED WITH OFFENSIVE SLOGANS

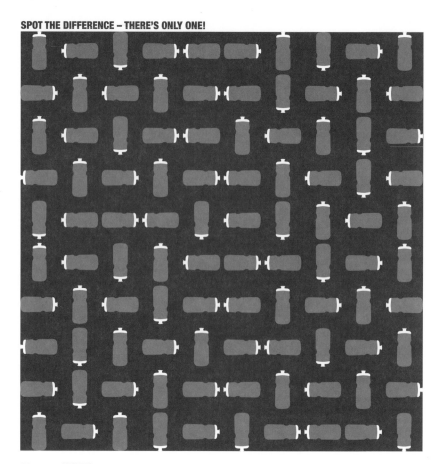

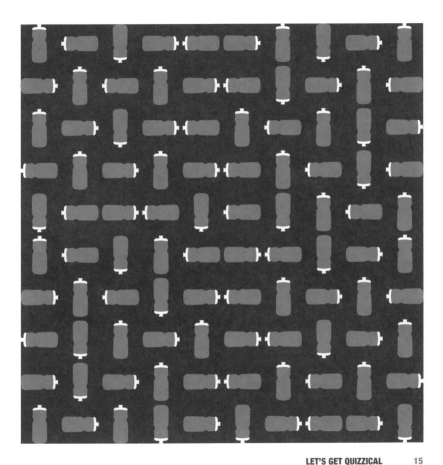

MPH

WHAT'S THE FASTEST RECORDED SPEED ANYBODY HAS EVER GONE ON A BICYCLE?

A) 92.7 MPH

B) 112.5 MPH

C) 152.2 MPH

THIS PAIR ONLY APPEARS ONCE
ON THE OPPOSITE PAGE

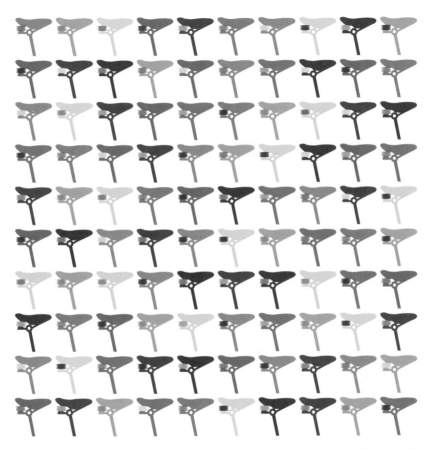

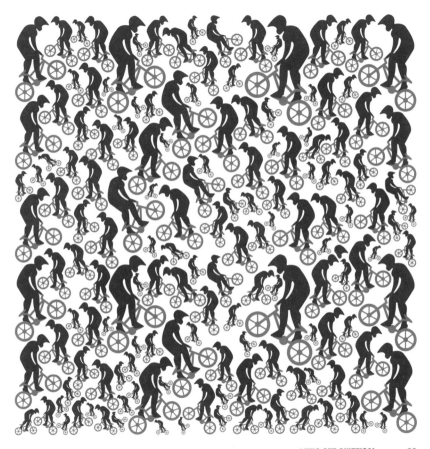

FIND THE 'PIT STOP'

THE MOST EXPENSIVE BICYCLE EVER SOLD FETCHED $500,000 AT SOTHEBY'S IN 2009. WHO WAS IT DESIGNED BY?

A) DAMIEN HIRST

B) THE WRIGHT BROTHERS

C) EDDY MERCKX

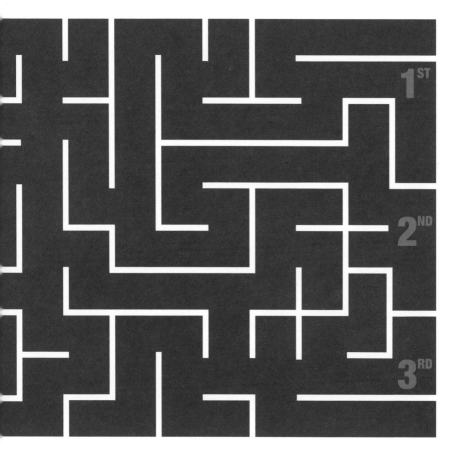

1ST

2ND

3RD

**THIS PAIR ONLY APPEARS ONCE
ON THE OPPOSITE PAGE**

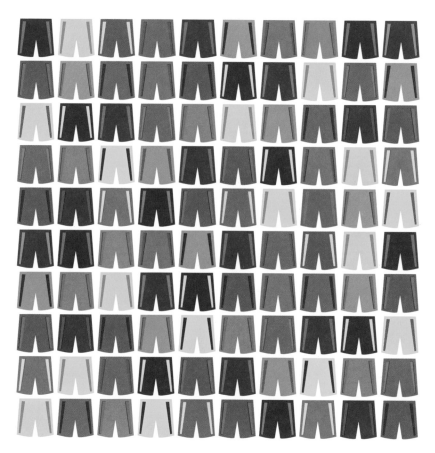

CANADIAN KRIS HOLM BROKE RECORDS BY BEING THE FIRST PERSON TO TRAVEL TO THE TOP OF CERTAIN VOLCANOES AND MOUNTAINS AROUND THE WORLD ON:

A) AN ELECTRIC BICYCLE

B) A PENNY-FARTHING

C) A UNICYCLE

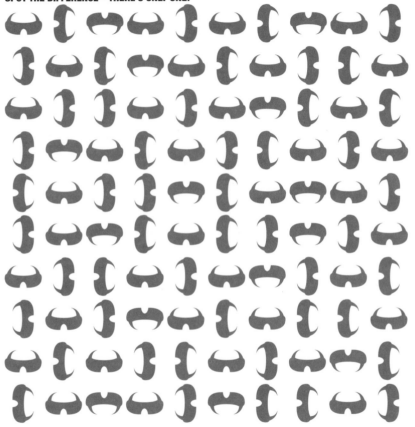

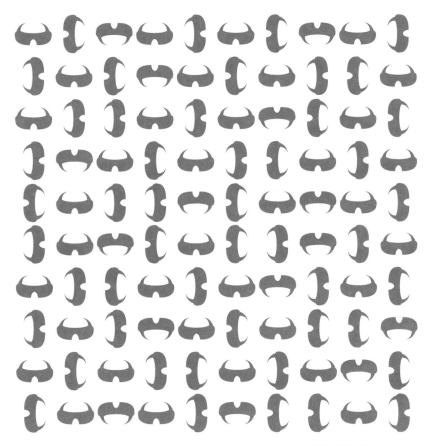

WHAT WERE BICYCLES CALLED BEFORE THE WORD WAS INVENTED IN THE 1860s?

A) WHEEL-O-GRAM

B) CYCLICADO

C) VELOCIPEDE

MOUNTAIN-BIKING LEGEND GARY FISHER WAS SUSPENDED FROM RACING AT THE AGE OF 17 DUE TO HIS:

A) LONG HAIR

B) NEON CYCLING CLOTHES

C) BAD ATTITUDE

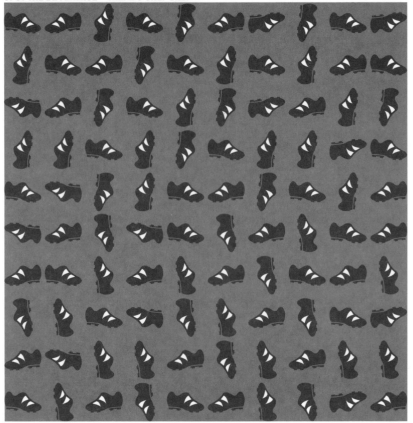

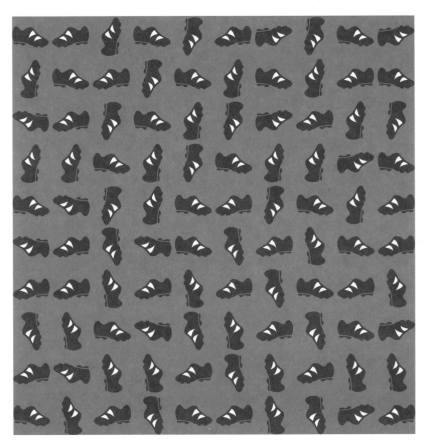

THIS PAIR ONLY APPEARS ONCE ON THE OPPOSITE PAGE

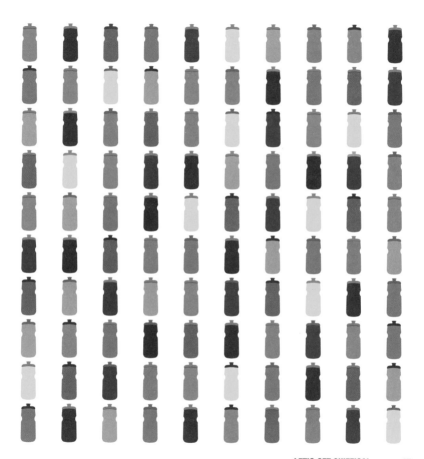

GET ME SOME WATER!

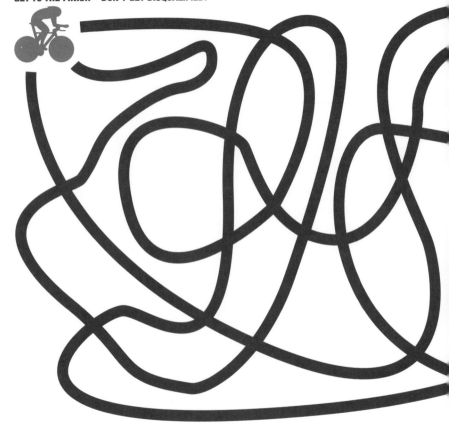

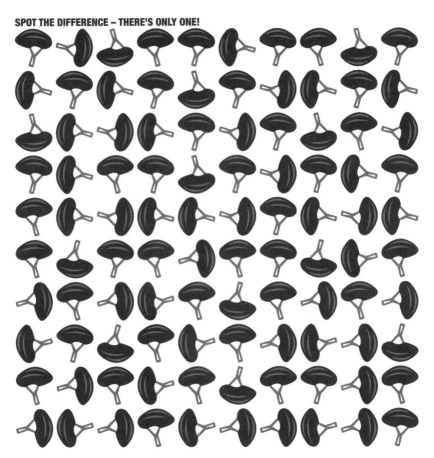

SHE WON! GIVE HER THE TROPHY!

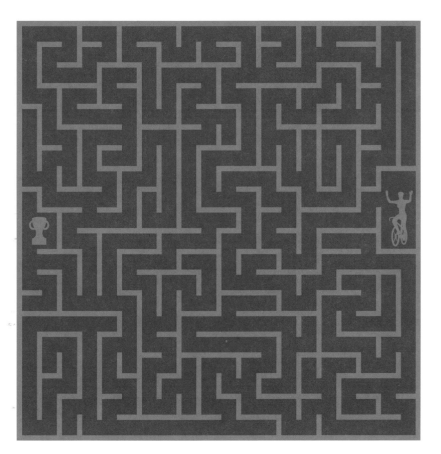

PUMP

PANNIER

RACK

LIGHT

BASKET

HELMET

GLOVES

REFLECTORS

BOTTLE

B E P P O I U F G S

P O R U S D T I R K

O I T R M G H O E L

U E F T A P T J I B

T G D E L C E T N M

R L S M E E K H N A

G O L L M N S G A S

F V F E H J A I P N

W E E H R T B L U L

R S S A Y D S G H P

IN 2009 ALBERTO CONTADOR WON
THE MOUNTAIN STAGE OF LE TOUR DE
FRANCE AND RECEIVED (ON TOP OF
THE PRIZE MONEY):

A) A RACING PIGEON

B) A ST BERNARD MOUNTAIN DOG

C) A MOUNTAIN EAGLE

SPOT THE DIFFERENCE – THERE'S ONLY ONE!

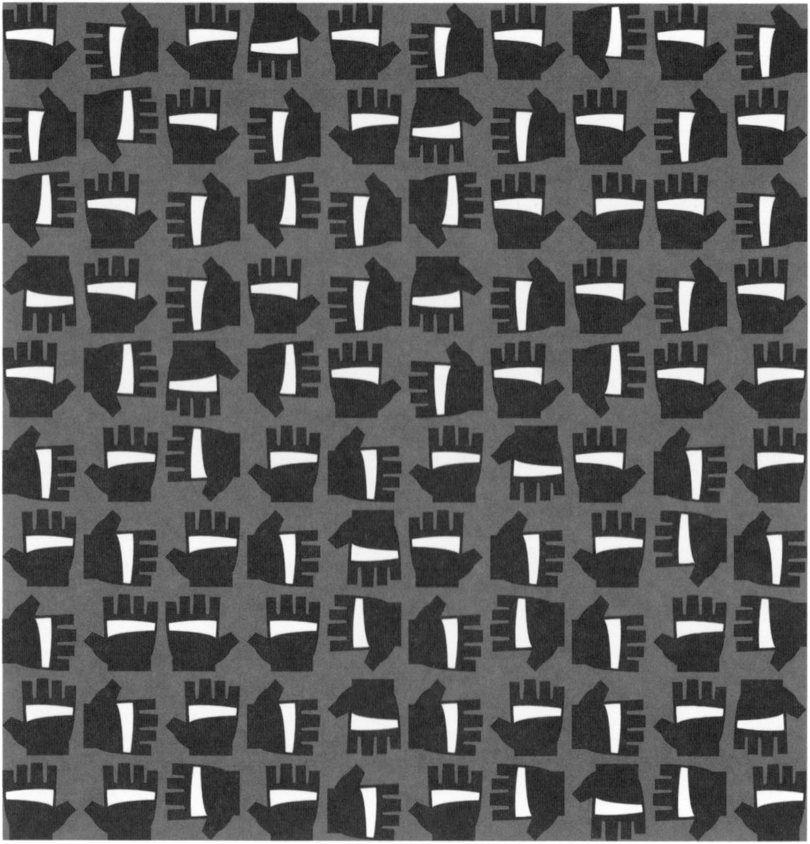

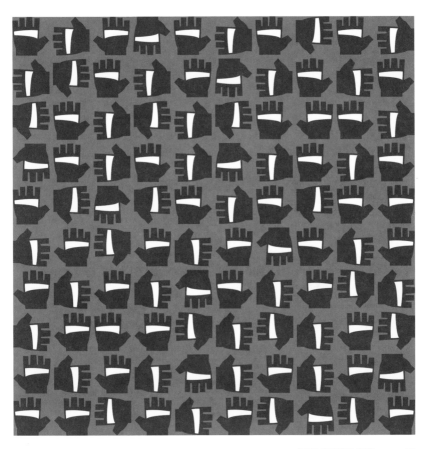

**THIS PAIR ONLY APPEARS ONCE
ON THE OPPOSITE PAGE**

FIND MY PENNY-FARTHING

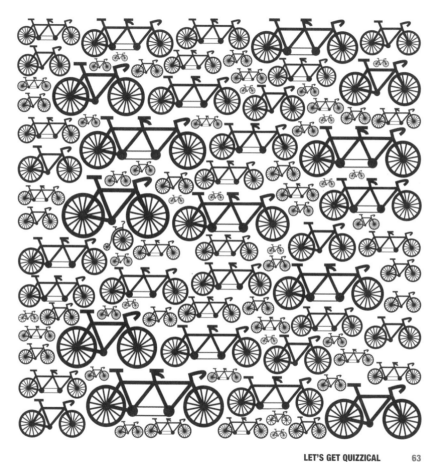

HURRY!
THE RACE STARTS IN FIVE MINUTES!

MECHANIC

LOUISON BOBET REFUSED TO WEAR THE YELLOW JERSEY DURING LE TOUR DE FRANCE BECAUSE:

A) IT DIDN'T GO WITH HIS SKIN TONE

B) ITS ARTIFICIAL YARN CONTENT WAS NOT HYGIENIC ENOUGH

C) YELLOW IS THE COLOUR OF COWARDICE

 **FIND THE BLUE CYCLING SHOE**

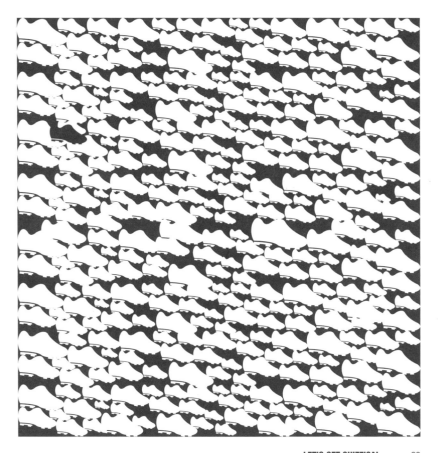

FROOME GREAT BRITAIN

OLIVER SPAIN

NIBALI ITALY

COOKE GREAT BRITAIN

DA COSTA PORTUGAL

MARTIN IRELAND

CANCELLARA SWITZERLAND

PORTE AUSTRALIA

PENDLETON GREAT BRITAIN

KREUZIGER CZECH REPUBLIC

CHAVANEL FRANCE

HORNER USA

```
B H C D A C O S T A
L A O L I V E R N R
E D I R F K E O E A
N L L K N J T G K L
A P A N O E I N O L
V O B M L Z R I O E
A R I D U P R T C C
H T N E W V U R S N
C E R Y A E I A T A
P K O F R O O M E C
```

WHICH OF THESE COUNTRIES HAS CYCLING AS ITS NATIONAL SPORT?

A) FRANCE

B) THE NETHERLANDS

C) ERITREA

**THIS PAIR ONLY APPEARS ONCE
ON THE OPPOSITE PAGE**

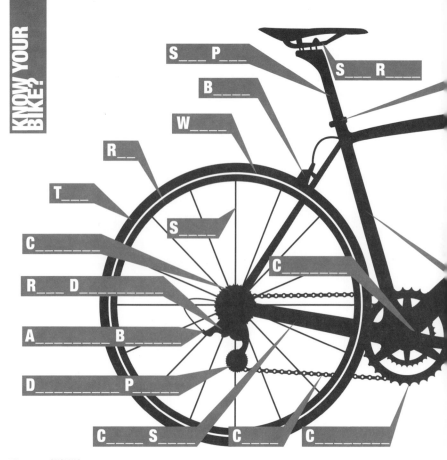

KNOW YOUR
BIKE?

S____ P____

S____ R____

B____

W____

R___

T____

C_____

S____

R____ D____

C_____

A_____ B____

D_____ P_____

C____ S____   C____   C____

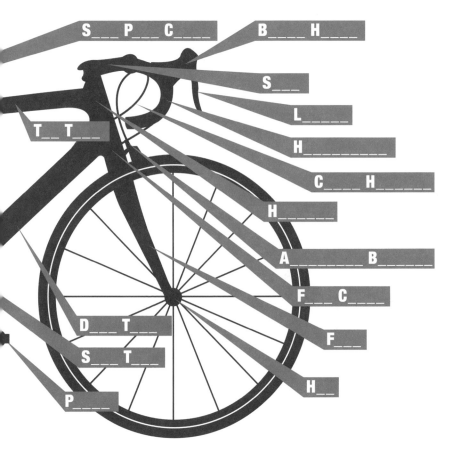

S_ _ _P_ _C_ _ _ _

B_ _ _ _H_ _ _ _ _

S_ _ _

L_ _ _ _ _

H_ _ _ _ _ _ _

C_ _ _ _H_ _ _ _ _ _

H_ _ _ _ _ _

A_ _ _ _ _ _B_ _ _ _ _ _

F_ _ _C_ _ _ _

F_ _ _

H_ _

T_ _T_ _ _ _

D_ _ _T_ _

S_ _ _T_ _

P_ _ _ _ _

SPOT THE DIFFERENCE – THERE'S ONLY ONE!

THERE ARE 1 BILLION BICYCLES IN THE WORLD, WHICH IS WHAT IN PROPORTION TO THE NUMBER OF CARS?

A) THE SAME AMOUNT

B) TWICE THE AMOUNT

C) FOUR TIMES THE AMOUNT

**THIS PAIR ONLY APPEARS ONCE
ON THE OPPOSITE PAGE**

RIDE ME TO THE RAMP!

ITALIANS USE BIKES FOR 5 PER CENT OF ALL TRIPS MADE, AND IN THE NETHERLANDS THIS FIGURE GOES UP TO 30 PER CENT. WHAT PERCENTAGE OF AMERICAN TRIPS ARE MADE ON BICYCLE?

A) 1 PER CENT

B) 4 PER CENT

C) 12 PER CENT

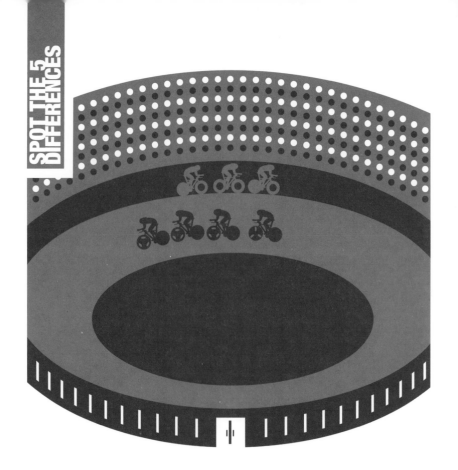

SPOT THE 5 DIFFERENCES

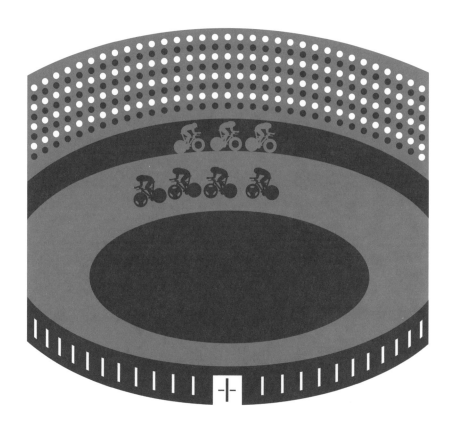

FIND THE BLUE WATER BOTTLE

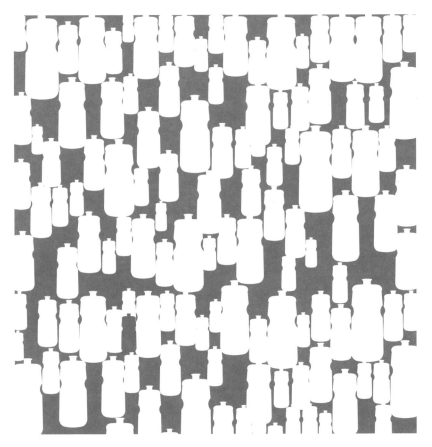

**THIS PAIR ONLY APPEARS ONCE
ON THE OPPOSITE PAGE**

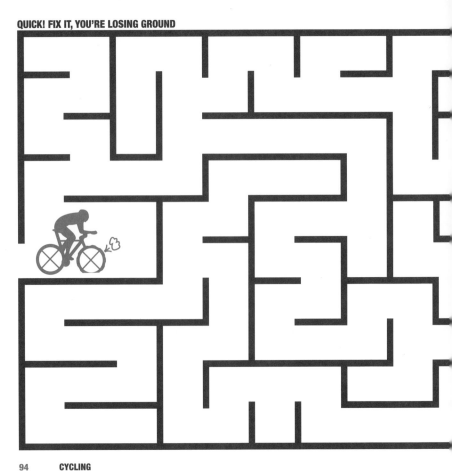

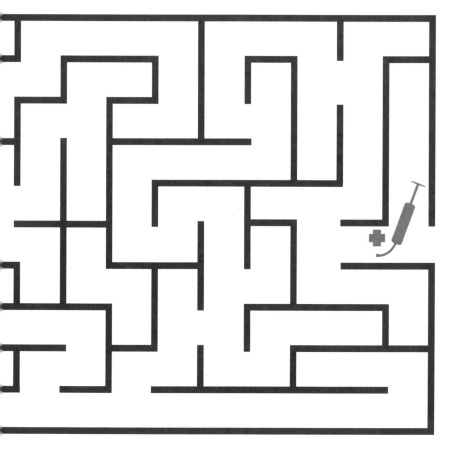

MARIS STROMBERGS BECAME THE FIRST OLYMPIC BMX RACING CHAMPION AT THE 2008 GAMES IN CHINA. WHICH COUNTRY DID HE REPRESENT?

A) LATVIA

B) AUSTRALIA

C) HUNGARY

BICYCLE TRICKS

BUNNY HOP
GRIND
TAILWHIP
AIR
THREE-SIXTY
LOOP OUT
VERT
RAMP
HALF-PIPE
BOWL
RAIL
FLATLAND

B	Y	F	G	N	M	A	S	I	E
M	T	L	X	R	B	O	W	L	P
T	X	A	O	A	I	R	P	O	I
R	I	T	I	G	H	N	H	O	P
E	S	L	B	N	X	Y	D	P	F
V	E	A	A	S	N	L	M	O	L
F	E	N	F	N	I	A	N	U	A
H	R	D	U	A	R	P	J	T	H
S	H	B	R	O	I	U	X	B	L
P	T	A	I	L	W	H	I	P	M

DUE TO ITS DISTINCTIVE SHAPE, WHAT IS THE VELODROME AT THE OLYMPIC PARK IN LONDON INFORMALLY KNOWN AS?

A) THE HAT

B) THE PRINGLE

C) THE SAUCER

ANSWERS

P4-5

P6-7

P8-9 C) 87.5

P10-11

P12-13 B) HIS EXTRA-MARITAL AFFAIR HAD BECOME PUBLIC

P14-15

P16-17

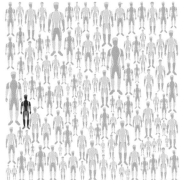

P18-19 C) 152.2 MPH

P20-21

P22-23

P24-25

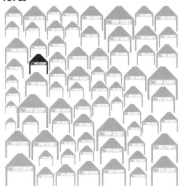

P26-27 A) DAMIEN HIRST

P28-29

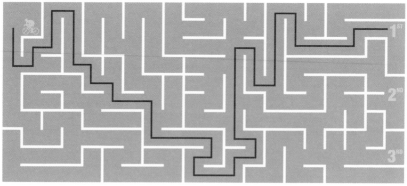

P32-33 C) A UNICYCLE

P30-31

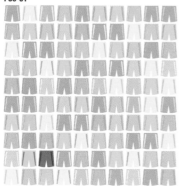

P34-35

P36-37 C) VELOCIPEDE

P38-39

P40-41 A) LONG HAIR

P42-43

P44-45

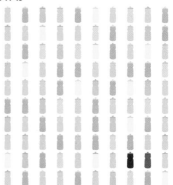

P46-47

P48–49

P50–51

P52–53

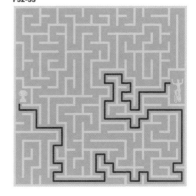

P56-57 B) A ST BERNARD MOUNTAIN DOG

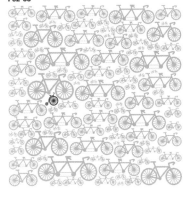

P66-67 B) ITS ARTIFICIAL YARN CONTENT WAS NOT HYGIENIC ENOUGH

P72-73 C) ERITREA

P68-69

P74-75

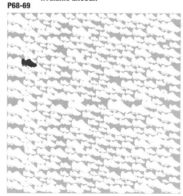

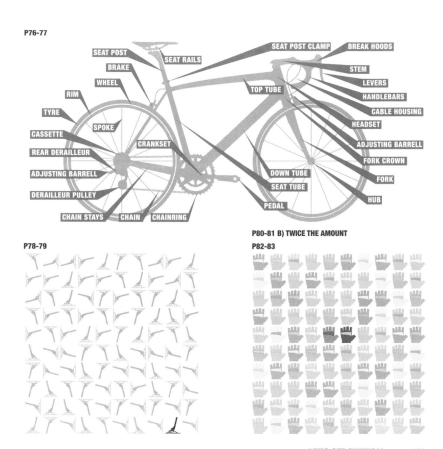

P76-77

SEAT POST
SEAT RAILS
BRAKE
WHEEL
RIM
TYRE
SPOKE
CASSETTE
REAR DERAILLEUR
CRANKSET
ADJUSTING BARRELL
DERAILLEUR PULLEY
CHAIN STAYS
CHAIN
CHAINRING

SEAT POST CLAMP
BREAK HOODS
STEM
LEVERS
HANDLEBARS
TOP TUBE
CABLE HOUSING
HEADSET
ADJUSTING BARRELL
FORK CROWN
DOWN TUBE
FORK
SEAT TUBE
PEDAL
HUB

P78-79

P80-81 B) TWICE THE AMOUNT

P82-83

P84-85

P86-87 A) 1 PER CENT

P88-89

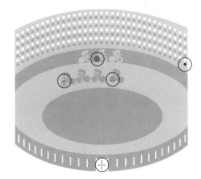

P90-91

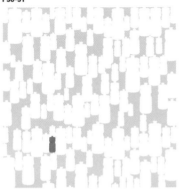

P92-93

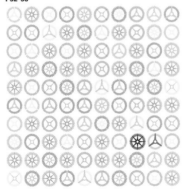

P94-95

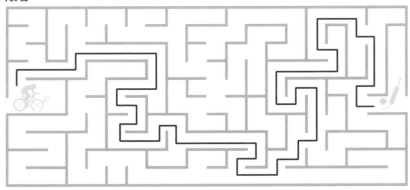

P96-97 A) LATVIA

P98-99

P100-101 B) THE PRINGLE

**IF YOU'RE INTERESTED IN FINDING OUT MORE ABOUT OUR BOOKS,
FIND US ON FACEBOOK AT** SUMMERSDALE PUBLISHERS **AND
FOLLOW US ON TWITTER AT** @SUMMERSDALE**.**

WWW.SUMMERSDALE.COM

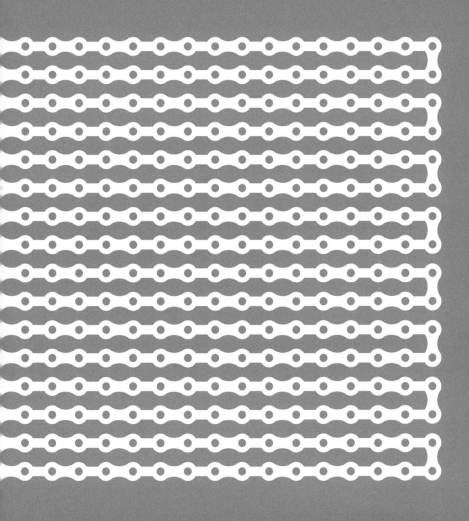

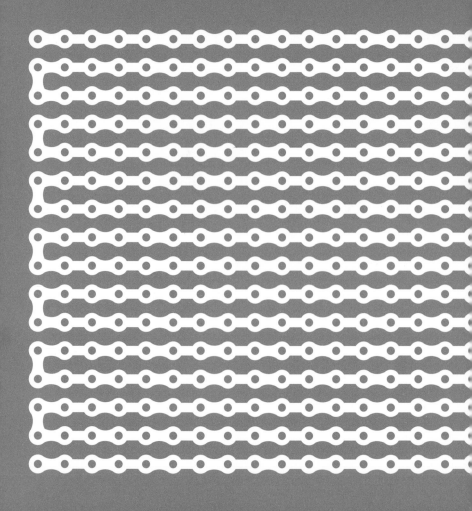